A Dorling Kindersley Book

Text Terry Martin
Project Editor Caroline Bingham
Senior Art Editor Sarah Wright-Smith
Deputy Managing Editor Mary Ling
Production Louise Barratt
Consultant Theresa Greenaway
Picture Researcher Lorna Ainger
Photography by Paul Bricknell, Matthew Chattle,
Andreas Einsiedel, Steve Gorton, Peter Powell,
Susannah Price, Tim Ridley, Steve Shott

First published in Great Britain in 1996
by Dorling Kindersley Limited,
9 Henrietta Street, London WC2E 8PS
4 6 8 10 9 7 5 3

A CIP catalogue record for this book
is available from the British Library.

ISBN: 0-7513-5460-0

Colour reproduction by Chromagraphics, Singapore
Printed and bound in Italy by L.E.G.O.

The publisher would like to thank the following
for their kind permission to reproduce their photographs:
t top, b bottom, l left, r right, c centre, BC back cover, FC front cover
Bruce Coleman Ltd.: Erwin & Peggy Bauer 14-15,
Jane Burton 11tr, 20-21c, Mr Felix Labhardt FC cr, BC cr, 5bl,
17tr, 21tr, Dr Scott Nielsen FC tl, BC tl, 11bc, Dr Eckart Pott 19tr,
John Shaw 20bl, Kim Taylor FC bl, BC bl, 5tr, 14tl, 18tl,bl, 19tl;
Robert Harding Picture Library: 18-19c, Fred Friberg 16-17c;
The Image Bank: Steve Dunwell 18-19, Eric Meola 15tl,
Pete Turner 12bl; Frank Lane Picture Agency: R.Bird 13br,
W.Broadhurst 21br, C.Carvalho 9tr; Photographer's Library:
19br; Pictor: 4c, 7br, 10tl,bl, 13tr, 17bl; Science Photo Library:
John Mead endpapers, Claude Nuridsany & Marie
Perennou FC cl, BC cl, 4tc,ca, 16-17; Tony Stone
Images: 6-7c, Beryl Bidwell 10-11c, Bert
Blokhuis 6tl, Val Corbett 18cl, George Hunter 8bl,
Richard Kaylin 12-13c, Gary Yeowell BC c, 8-9c.

Contents

WHY

does lightning strike?

Questions children ask
about the weather

DK

DORLING KINDERSLEY
London • New York • Stuttgart • Moscow

Why is the sun hot?

The sun is a ball of burning gases. We feel its heat on Earth, even though it's 150 million km away.

Why can't I look at the sun?
The sun is much too bright for our delicate eyes, and could cause blindness. It's rude to stare – and in this case, it's very dangerous.

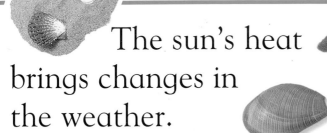

The sun's heat brings changes in the weather.

Why does it feel cold when a cloud covers the sun?
Clouds soak up most of the sun's warm rays, just like a sponge soaks up water. The air near the ground soon cools, and this can spoil your fun in the sun.

7

Why do rainbows

Rainbows appear when the sun is behind you and it's raining ahead of you. The sunlight splits into colours as it passes through water droplets.

Why are rainbows full of colour?
White sunlight is a perfect blend of seven colours: red, orange, yellow,

appear?

Why is this rainbow white? In the cold, white Arctic, the sun creates the most amazing sights. This icebow forms when sunlight passes through falling ice crystals. These keep the sun's white rays together.

green, blue, indigo and violet. So these are the colours that appear when a ray of sunlight is split up as it passes through a raindrop.

Why does it rain?

Clouds hold the answer. They carry tiny water droplets which bump into each other, growing bigger and heavier, until ... "look out below", and down comes the rain.

Why do clouds appear?
When warm air rises to meet cold air, moisture in the warm air condenses to make water droplets.

Why do rain-clouds look so dark?

Many rain-clouds appear quite dark. This is caused by the density of water droplets in each part of the cloud. The cloud may be several kilometres thick.

These tiny droplets reflect sunlight, and a fluffy cloud appears.

Why does lightning

A lightning bolt is a giant spark of electricity. It strikes because it is attracted to the ground, in the same way that a magnet attracts certain metals.

Why is thunder so noisy?
The loud crashes of a heavy thunderstorm happen because the scorching hot lightning makes the air expand too fast. That makes a big boom.

strike?

Why does thunder follow lightning?
Flash! Silence. Kerboom! Thunder and lightning occur at the same time, but sound travels more slowly than light.

Why shouldn't I shelter under a tree?
When lightning strikes a tree, the electricity shoots down the trunk. It may electrocute you if you are too close.

Why does the

Wind is whistling, invisible air. It blows because air never stops moving – warm air always rises, and cold air rushes in to take its place.

Why do kites fly?

Kites are made to fly "up, up and away" on windy days. The stretched material is caught by the wind, and pulled up. Hold the string tight!

wind blow?

It's like a game of chase that never stops, but gets faster or slower.

Why do tornadoes appear?
Tornadoes spiral up when a funnel of hot, damp air meets cold, dry air. They are dangerous whirlwinds, and they suck up everything in their path.

Why does it snow?

Clouds can get so cold, their water droplets freeze into tiny ice crystals. The crystals cling to each other as they fall from the sky, turning into soft snowflakes.

Why is a snowflake star-shaped? It isn't! It's made up of about 50 tiny crystals that are. Each crystal has six sides, and no two are the same. You can only see the crystals through a microscope.

Why does a snowman take so long to melt? Snow reflects the sun's heat and light. When it is squashed tightly together, as in a snowman's body, it can re-freeze as temperatures drop overnight, and so last for days or weeks.

Why is ice slippery?

When skating across ice, your weight melts the top layer, creating a slippery surface between your skates and the ice.

Why do leaves get frosty?
Water in the air freezes on a cold, solid surface – such as a leaf or flower. This is known as hoar frost.

Why do icicles appear?
Spikes of ice slowly grow when drops of water freeze before they can drip to the ground.

Why are icebergs so big?
An iceberg is a broken-off bit of glacier that floats in the sea. The floating crystal castle is just the tip of the iceberg. The rest of it is hidden under the water.

Why do dewdrops appear

As the night air cools, the moisture it contains condenses into droplets. By morning, these droplets are clinging to all sorts of things, from spiders' webs to insects' wings.

Why do we have mist?
Just like dew, mist appears when water in the air condenses into

overnight?

Why is fog thick?
Fog is thicker than mist. It contains many more water droplets. In cities these can pick up dust and dirt from cars and smoke.

droplets. This makes a cloud appear – but at ground level, so you can walk right through it!